Our Earth

RIVERS

Terry Jennings

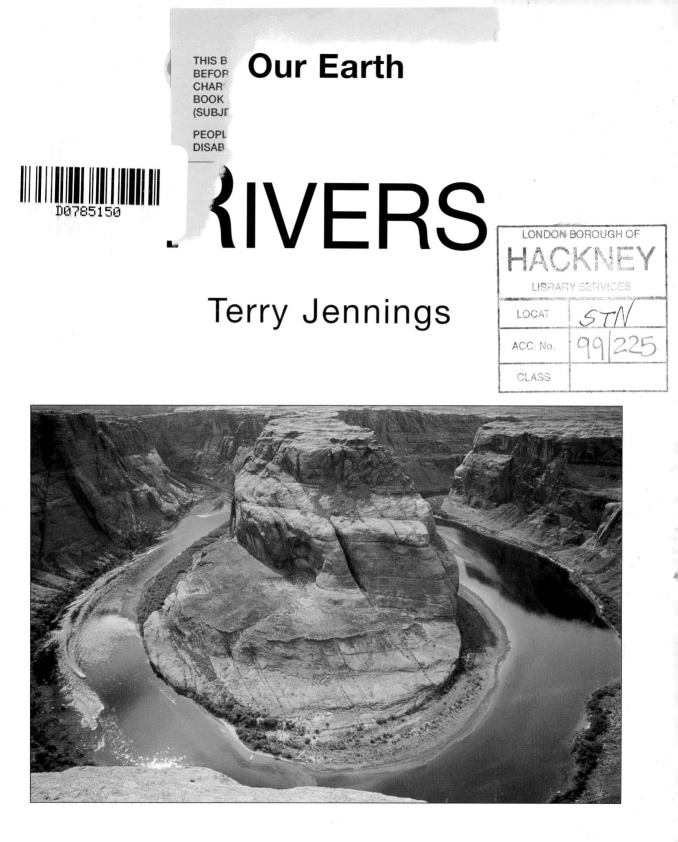

First published in Great Britain in 1999 by
 Belitha Press Limited,
London House, Great Eastern Wharf,
Parkgate Road, London SW11 4NQ

Editor Honor Head
Designer Helen James
Illustrator Graham Rosewarne
Picture researcher Diana Morris

ISBN 1 85561 882 6 (hardback)
ISBN 1 84138 034 2 (paperback)
ISBN 1 84138 028 8 (Big Book)

Printed in Hong Kong

British Library Cataloguing in Publication Data
CIP data for this book is available from the British Library

Photographic credits

J. Allan Cash: 4b, 7b, 11b, 19t, 20t, 22, 23, 28t. **James Davis Photography**: 4t, 26t.
Eye Ubiquitous: 13 **Julia Waterlow. Getty Images**: front cover **Chad Ehlers.**
Terry Jennings: 7t, 12b, 14, 19b. **Frank Lane Picture Agency**: 8 **W. Wisniewski**,
9 **Hans Dieter Brandl**, 25t **W. Wisniewski. NASA**: 15b. **Still Pictures**: title page,
10 **Brookshier-UNEP**, 5 **André Bartschi**, 26b **Gerard and Margi Moss**, 28b **Jean-Luc
Zeiger. Trip**: 17b **W. Jacobs**, 18t **Dinodia. Zefa**: 17t, 18b, 21 **Werbestudio**, 25b **Horus**, 27.

Cover Usumacinta River, Guatemala

Words in **bold** appear in the glossary on pages 30 and 31.

Contents

What is a river?

A river is water which flows towards the sea, a lake or another river. Most rivers start high in the hills or mountains.

We need rivers

Most of our water comes from rivers. We need clean water for drinking, cooking and washing. Lots of plants and animals live in rivers.

▲ *The River Nile in Africa is the longest river in the world. The sailing boats carry cargo along the river.*

▶ *The water in the River Ganges in India is used for cooking, washing and cleaning clothes.*

Looking at rivers

In this book we find out how rivers are made. We see how they grow and how they change the land around them. We also look at some of the animals and plants that live in rivers and learn why rivers are important to people.

▲ *The River Amazon in Brazil flows through thick **rainforest**.*

Where rivers begin

▼ *Rivers are part of the water cycle. The water cycle lets us use the same water over and over again.*

The water in rivers comes from rain or snow. When rain falls on the land, or snow melts, some of the water trickles over the ground. These trickles join up to form tiny streams. The streams become bigger and make rivers.

as clouds pass over the mountains, they cool and it rains

the rain falls into the river and flows down to the sea

clouds

heat from the sun

river

water from the rivers and sea warms up and turns into clouds

sea

Springs

Some water from rain or melted snow soaks into the ground. The water passes through the ground until it flows out of the side of a hill or mountain. This is called a spring. Some springs flow all the time. Others flow only when it rains.

▲ *Many rivers begin as a tiny spring like this. Springs are formed when water comes out of the ground.*

New rivers

Not all rivers start from streams and springs. Some rivers flow from lakes. Others come from the ends of melting glaciers. Glaciers are rivers of ice that form high in the mountains.

◄ *This glacier in Canada is the beginning or source of the River Athabaska.*

Joining up

From its beginning, or source, a stream flows quickly downhill. It may become bigger and flow faster after heavy rain or snow.

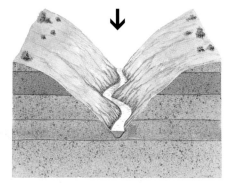

Wearing away

Streams carry along tiny pieces of rock, pebbles and large boulders. These wear away the bottom and sides of the stream, making it deeper and wider. Gradually the stream carves out a **valley**.

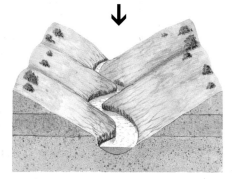

▲ How a stream slowly wears away the ground to make a valley.

► The water in this stream in Norway rushes down a mountain slope.

Growing bigger

A river grows bigger as it is joined by streams and other small rivers. These are called **tributaries**. The more water the river has, the larger the valley it makes.

Sand, gravel and mud

Stones and lumps of rock in the river bump into each other. Pieces break off and form gravel, sand and mud. These are swept along by the water.

▼ *The Grand Canyon in the United States is a deep valley which was made by the Colorado River.*

Deeper and wider

▲ *This huge bend or meander on the Colorado River in the United States almost makes a complete circle.*

A river becomes deeper and wider when it gets closer to the sea. This is because more and more tributaries join it. Tributaries bring water to the river from other parts of the land.

Slowing down

Once a river leaves the hills or mountains it flows more slowly. The river becomes wider and is lined with sand and small pebbles. Water plants can grow in the river because the **current** is not strong enough to wash them away.

Round the bend

When the river flows more slowly the water is no longer strong enough to rush over large rocks in its way. Instead it flows round them and bends from side to side. These twists and bends are called **meanders**. As the river twists and bends the water wears away the **banks**. Bits of rock and sand break off from the bank and are carried along by the water.

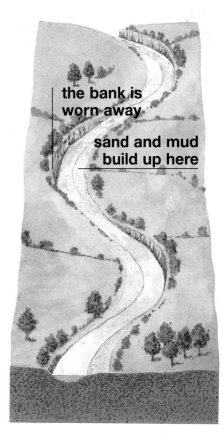

the bank is worn away

sand and mud build up here

▲ *How a river makes bends or meanders.*

▶ *The water in this river looks dark because of all the mud and sand it is carrying.*

Flowing along

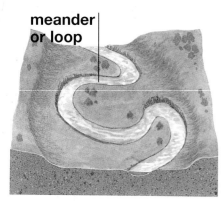

meander or loop

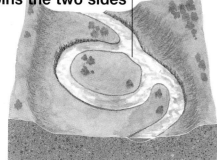

flooding water joins the two sides

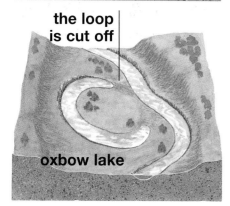

the loop is cut off

oxbow lake

▲ *An oxbow lake is formed when a river cuts off one of its own meanders or loops.*

▶ *A long oxbow lake by a river in Wales.*

Where a river nears the sea, it twists and turns and flows more slowly.

Oxbow lakes

A slow-moving river makes huge meanders or loops around obstacles. When the river **floods**, water flows across the land between the two sides of the river. This cuts off the loop or meander and leaves behind a lake. This is called an oxbow lake.

River banks

When the river flows very slowly the mud and sand it is carrying drops along the sides. This makes sand and mud banks. The river flows between these banks.

▲ *This **canal** has been dug next to the River Nile in Africa. Farmers use it to water the soil so that they can grow crops such as wheat, rice and vegetables.*

Flooding the land

When the river floods, water pours over its banks. It spreads mud and sand over the valley. This mud and sand makes the soil very **fertile**.

Down to the sea

▲ *This is a salt marsh made from mud and sand from the river.*

The mouth of the river is where it meets the sea. All rivers that flow into a lake or the sea carry a lot of fine mud and sand with them. As the river flows into the sea it drops its mud and sand. Much of this is carried away by the sea. But in some areas mud and sand builds up to form **salt marshes**.

Making land

In places where there are no strong currents, fine mud and sand are dropped at the river's mouth. This makes a muddy piece of land called a delta. A delta is shaped like a triangle.

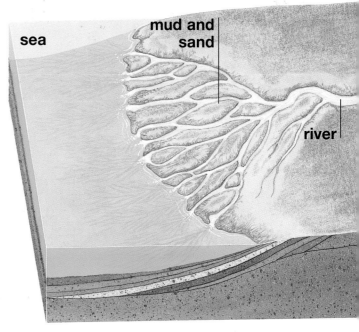

▲ *The river makes banks of mud and sand called deltas. The water flows through them to the sea.*

Farm land

Large deltas, such as those at the River Ganges and River Nile, provide some of the most fertile land in the world. Here farmers grow food crops such as wheat, rice and vegetables.

◀ *This is the delta of the River Nile in Egypt, seen from a **satellite** in space.*

Waterfalls

Most waterfalls are made by rivers in the mountains.

Falling water

Sometimes a layer of hard rock lies on top of a layer of soft rock. The river wears away the soft rock much faster than the hard rock. This leaves a ledge or step of hard rock. The river falls over the ledge, making a waterfall.

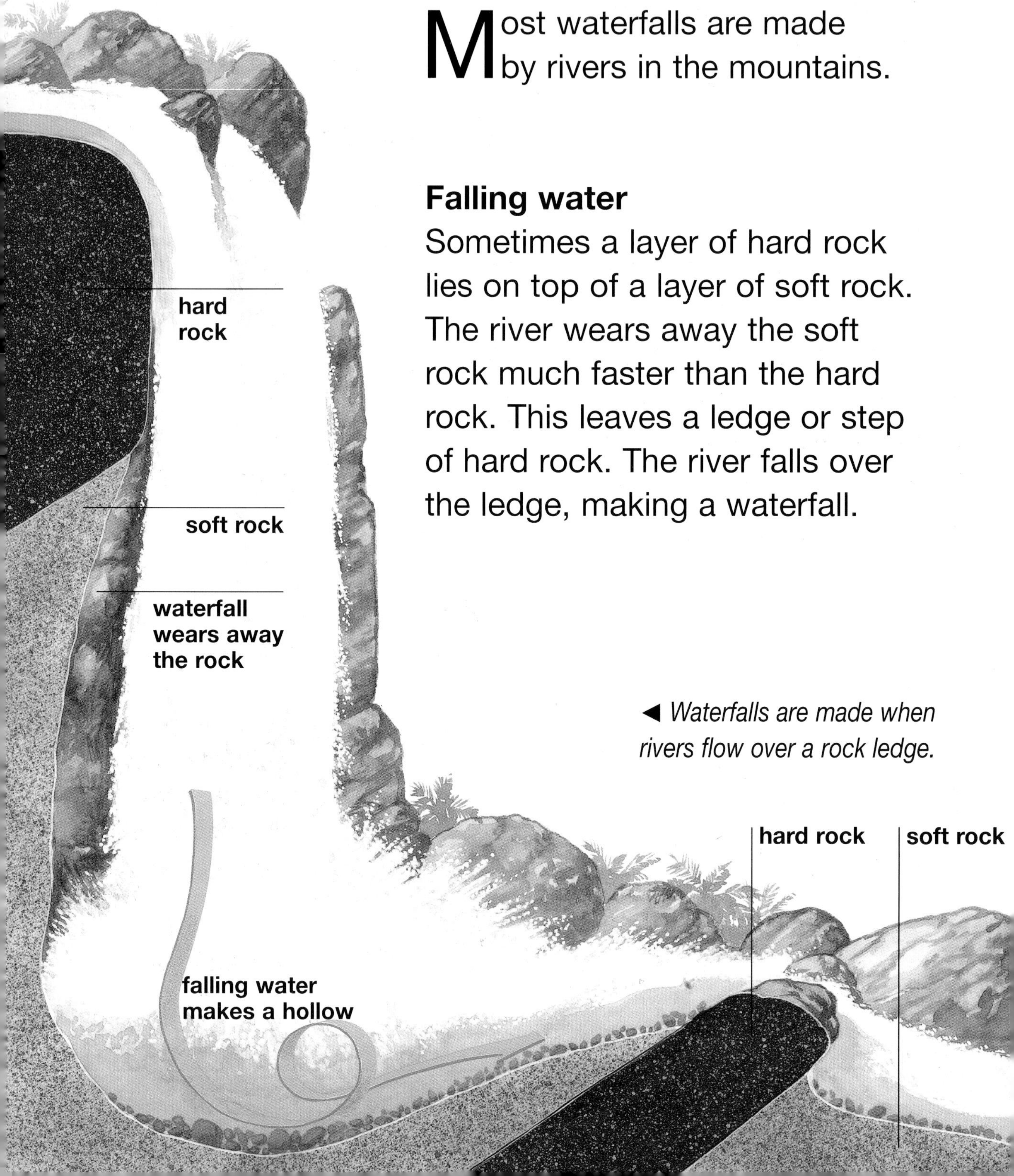

hard rock

soft rock

waterfall wears away the rock

◄ *Waterfalls are made when rivers flow over a rock ledge.*

hard rock | soft rock

falling water makes a hollow

Moving waterfalls

The water falling over the rock ledge gradually wears away the rock. As this happens, the falling water moves back.

Small waterfalls

If a river bed has layers of hard and soft rocks, the soft rocks wear away to make a series of hard rock steps. The river then flows over these steps, making small waterfalls, called **rapids**.

▲ *The Angel Falls in South America are the highest waterfalls in the world.*

◄ *People use rubber boats to travel over the rapids in a fast-flowing river.*

Floods

A river floods when heavy rainfall or melting snow produces more water than the river can hold.

▲ *A flooded street in Bombay in India.*

Bigger beds

Some river beds become built up with mud and sand. This is happening in the Mississippi River in the United States. As the river bed becomes higher, the people have to build high banks to stop the river flooding.

▼ *The Thames Barrier in London is a dam which helps to stop the river flooding.*

Dangerous floods

When the Huang He river in China flooded in 1935, four million people lost their homes. High banks were built on either side of the river to try to stop the floods.

Ice blocks

In cold countries, rivers freeze over in winter. In the spring, if the ice near the river's mouth doesn't melt quickly enough, the water cannot flow out to sea.

▲ *Removing mud and sand from the bottom of a river to stop it flooding.*

Stopping floods

Some kinds of flooding can be stopped by building a **dam** across the river. This holds back the river water and forms a lake called a **reservoir**. The water then flows slowly through the dam to avoid floods.

◄ *This dam and reservoir stop the river flooding.*

Underground rivers

Some rocks are so hard that water runs over them. Other rocks, such as chalk and limestone, are softer and soak up water.

Disappearing rivers

There are not many rivers where there are limestone rocks. This is because the river disappears down holes in the limestone. It flows underground and reappears at the foot of the hill or mountain.

▲ A **potholer** exploring an underground cave and river.

▼ In limestone areas, rivers often disappear underground.

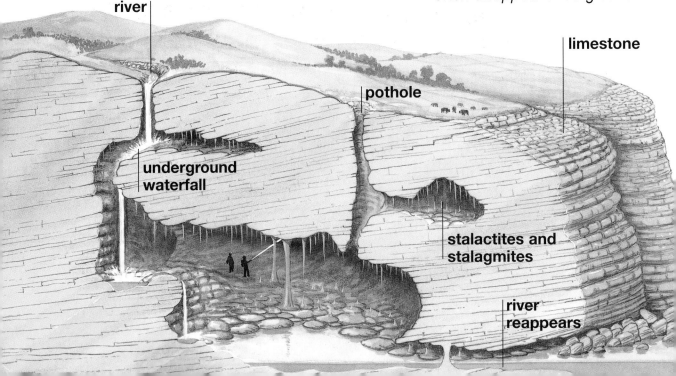

river

limestone

pothole

underground waterfall

stalactites and stalagmites

river reappears

▶ *Stalactites and stalagmites are many different shapes, sizes and colours. Sometimes they join together to make a limestone pillar.*

Dark caves

Limestone has many cracks running through it. Rain makes these cracks wider, because rainwater is a very weak **acid**. Eventually the cracks get so big they form underground caves and tunnels. Rivers flow through holes in the ground into these caves and travel underground.

Shining spikes

Many caves contain shining spikes of limestone called stalactites and stalagmites. Stalactites hang down from the roof like icicles. Stalagmites point up from the floor. They are made when water containing limestone drips from the cave roof. It takes hundreds of years for them to form.

Water at work

People have always used water to help them in their work. Today, factories and **power stations** use huge amounts of water.

▲ *This simple water wheel is made of wood. When water runs over the blades, the wheel turns.*

Water wheels

The water wheel was the first invention to use the power of water. The first water wheels were used to grind corn to make flour.

Water for electricity

Water power is used to supply electricity to large areas. Electricity made by the force of running water is called **hydro-electricity**. It is used in mountain areas where there are fast-flowing rivers.

Dams and reservoirs

Most hydro-electric power stations are built where there are high dams. Water is stored in a reservoir behind the dam. Some of this water is piped to houses and factories and some is used to water crops. Some of the water is used to turn modern water wheels, called **turbines**. These turn the **generators** that make electricity.

▲ *Holiday-makers travel by boat along the River Rhine in Germany.*

▼ *In a hydro-electric power station flowing water turns the turbines. These turn the generators that make electricity.*

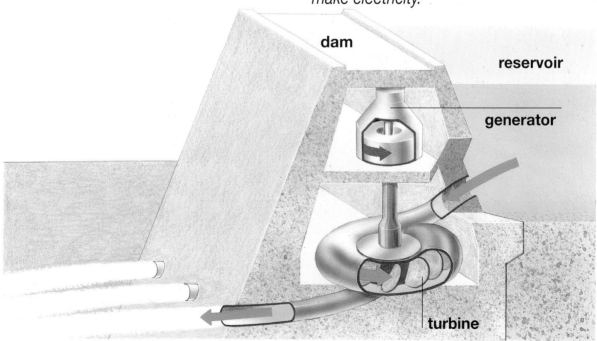

dam

reservoir

generator

turbine

River wildlife

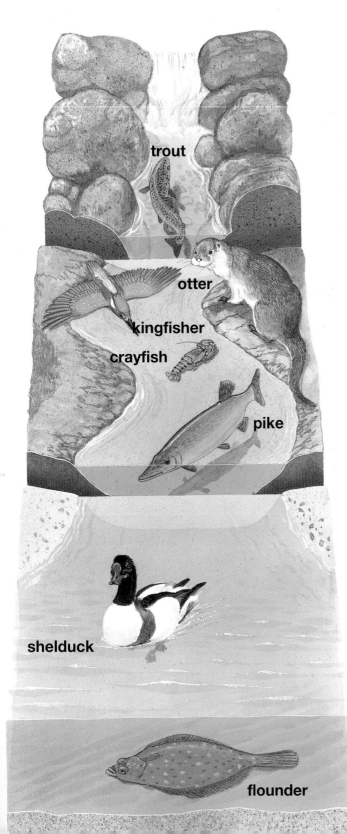

Many plants and animals live in or near rivers.

River animals

At the start of a river the water is usually cold, clear and fast-flowing. Not many plants or animals live there. Some fish, such as trout, can swim against the strong currents. Other animals, such as crayfish, water shrimps and many insects, live further down the river. These are eaten by fish, including minnows and salmon. These fish are then eaten by larger birds and animals such as kingfishers, herons and otters.

◄ *Different animals live in different parts of a river.*

◀ *The hippopotamus lives and feeds in rivers in Africa. It only comes on to land at night.*

Along the river

As the river grows bigger, plants grow in it. Fish, such as bream, perch and pike, live here. The end of the river is where it meets the sea and fresh water mixes with sea water. Some fish, such as flounders, live here.

More animals

Big animals, as well as fish, live in **tropical rivers**. These include crocodiles, anacondas (the world's biggest snake) and hippopotamuses. Many other animals visit the river to drink and swim.

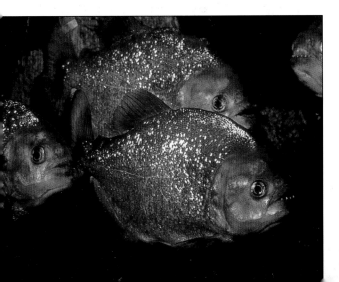

◀ *These piranha fish live in the tropical River Amazon. They have razor-sharp teeth to attack fish and wounded and sick animals in the water.*

Life by the river

▲ *A boy fishing in a river in Indonesia. River fish are an important food for many people.*

Millions of people live beside rivers. Even more people use river water for drinking, washing and cooking. Water is taken from rivers to water crops in fields. This is called **irrigation**.

Towns and cities

Most towns and cities grew from villages built beside rivers. People and animals use the water, and crops grow well on the land beside a river. Rivers make it easy to move goods and people by boat or ship.

◀ *These houses in Thailand are built on stilts to avoid floods and water snakes.*

Crossing the river

Many towns grew up by a river where a bridge could be built. Others grew up at a **ford** where the river was shallow enough to be crossed safely on foot.

Roads and railways

In the past people used rivers for travel because there were no roads. Many roads and railways were built beside rivers because the ground there is flat.

▼ *Roads and railways have been built along the River Mosel in Germany.*

Cleaner rivers

There are many towns and cities near rivers. Unfortunately, people are making rivers dirty or **polluted**.

▲ Litter harms wildlife and makes rivers unsafe for humans to use.

Washing away wastes

Towns, factories and farms put **sewage** and poisonous chemicals into rivers. This kills river plants and animals and makes the water unsafe for people to use.

Acid rain

Gas from chimneys, cars and lorries make **acid rain**. This may fall a long way away from the roads and factories. Acid rain is killing fish in many rivers.

◄ These fish died because the river was polluted.

Cleaning up

Many countries have laws to stop rivers being polluted. Factories have to clean their wastes instead of dumping them straight into rivers. Sewage is made safe at **sewage works** before it is put into rivers. Cars, power stations and factories have to clean the gas they put into the air. This means that there is less acid rain.

Cleaner rivers

Where there are laws to protect rivers, the water is now cleaner. Fish, birds and other kinds of wildlife have come back to live there. The water is also safe for people to use.

▶ The main ways in which a river becomes polluted.

acid rain

gas from factories and power stations

old sewage works

oil refineries

farm chemicals and animal manure

oil tankers

oil slick

sewage from the city

Glossary

acid A liquid chemical which burns.

acid rain Rain that contains harmful acids that come from gases from factories and cars.

bank The high ground beside a river.

canal A man-made waterway.

current The flow of water in a particular direction.

dam A large wall built to hold back water. A large lake called a reservoir is formed behind the dam.

fertile Land that is fertile has soil which is good for crops.

flood A river floods when the water flows over its banks.

ford A place where a river is shallow and can be easily crossed.

generator A machine which turns to make electricity.

hydro-electricity Electricity which is made using running water.

irrigation Watering dry land so that crops will grow.

meander A bend or twist in a river.

pollute To dirty the air, water or soil with rubbish and waste.

pothole A small hole which leads down under the ground into a cave.

power station A place where electricity is made.

rainforest Thick forest which grows where it is hot and there is lots of rain.

rapids Part of a river where the water flows very quickly over rocks.

reservoir A large lake which is made when a dam is built.

salt marsh Banks of mud in a river where the river runs into the sea. This is where fresh water and salt water meet.

satellite A camera in space which takes photographs of the Earth.

sewage Waste material from houses and factories, carried away by drains or sewers.

sewage works Places where dirty water is cleaned so that it can be put back into rivers or sometimes into the sea.

tributary A river or stream which flows into another larger river or stream.

turbine A kind of wheel which is turned by flowing water.

tropical rivers Rivers in the tropics. These are places where it is very hot and wet.

valley A strip of land between steep hills or mountains.

Index

bold = a picture reference